MIRACLE LIFE

Yvette Stembridge

MIRACLE LIFE

Scripture quotations are taken from The Holy Bible,
New International Version® (NIV®),
copyright © 1973, 1978, 1984 by the International Bible Society.
Used by permission. All rights reserved.

Bible Society of South Africa. (1978).
The Holy Bible, New International Version.
Cape Town, South Africa.

First published 2026

Published by Yvette Stembridge using Authors Crew services
Edited by Rodger Schippel and Margaret Sinclair for Authors Crew.
Cover design by Authors Crew.
Website: www.authorscrew.com
Email: info@authorscrew.com
Printed and bound in South Africa

This book is dedicated to:

My husband Ross.
Thank you for your love, care and partnership,
and for taking this life adventure with me.

To my loving and wonderful children and spouses
Tammy and Darren, Craig and Brittany, Nick and Michaela—
my constant support and encouragement.
I love you all.

Special Thanks

Thank you to God for always being by my side. For picking me up, dusting me off, and keeping His promises.

To all those I have met along my journey — you have each given a piece of yourselves and left a lasting impression on me. This has formed who I am today. Thank you.

Table of Contents

Introduction

2012 — As I lay on my bed staring out the window at the glistening turquoise sea, with seagulls hovering above each wave in hope of an early morning snack of sardines, my mind wandered and I asked myself: why has God not healed me this time? He has in the past. I knew what He was capable of. I had the evidence of it written across the whole arc of my life. And yet here I was, totally bedridden, watching the world carry on through a pane of glass I could not reach. I had returned to South Africa after being diagnosed in the UK with catastrophic Antiphospholipid Syndrome.

I had been managing a private hospital in Durban, South Africa, and had been transferred as Executive Director to their biggest hospital in the UK. It was a position I had worked toward for years, and I had thrown myself into it with the energy and determination that had carried me through every challenge before it. I had been working in the UK for a year. It was 2011, and I was attending a conference for all the Executive Directors. The day had been unremarkable. Meetings, discussions, the usual business of running a large institution. That night, however, everything changed.

I developed the most excruciating pain in my lung area. I was writing on the floor of my hotel room. Perspiration poured off my forehead. I gasped for air, each breath feeling as though it were being drawn through a passage that was rapidly closing. Then the vomiting of fresh blood started. The carpet beneath me turned dark. To this day I do not know how I survived that night. I was in agony — so much so that I could not even think of being frightened, as I was so focused on breathing and managing the pain. Fear requires a certain amount of spare capacity, and I had none. Every ounce of my being was directed toward the simple mechanics of staying alive until morning.

The next morning I contacted my personal assistant and told her I was on the way to the hospital and to please ask my general practitioner, based at the hospital, to be ready for me. I dragged myself to the car and slumped into the seat.

How was I going to drive? The steering wheel seemed impossibly far away, and the act of turning a key felt like it required strength I did not possess. I said a prayer and started the car. Thankfully it was an automatic. I was not very far from my hospital. I arrived, and the Operations Manager was waiting in the car park for me. I managed to heave myself out of the low seat of my cabriolet, took a few steps, and collapsed in her arms.

I was taken straight to the imaging department, where the team ushered me into the room for a CT scan. My doctor was waiting for me. The CT scan revealed multiple bilateral pulmonary emboli — blood clots in both lungs. I was wheeled to the small intensive care unit. Everyone shot into action. It was the weekend. Usually the hospital did not house anyone over the weekend in intensive care due to the unavailability of trained staff. An order was received from the national management to transfer me to an NHS hospital intensive care unit.

The message that came through was: "We can't afford to have our own ED die in her own hospital." There was a grim practicality to those words that I might have found darkly amusing under different circumstances. By evening I found myself in a very big NHS hospital general ward, as when we arrived the intensive care unit did not have the promised bed available. It did not take the staff very long to realise this was no ordinary general ward admission, and I was moved to a side ward directly opposite the nurses' station. After having nursed for many years when I was younger, as an intensive care nurse, I knew — as all medical staff know — that once you are put into the side ward next to the nurses' station, your prospects of survival look rather bleak. That room is where they put you when they want to keep a close eye on your departure from this world.

Night came and a new set of staff came on duty. It was evident they were very short-staffed. The night registered nurse heading the shift came into my room. She looked frantic. I could tell that her evening was already off to a bad start and it was still early. She had too many patients, too few hands, and a long night stretching ahead of her. She said goodnight and gently closed my door. That would be the last face I would see until morning. They were evidently too busy, too short-staffed, and chose to give their attention to patients who had a fighting chance. Obviously, according to their assessment, that was not me. I was already on my way out.

It was one of the longest nights of my life. The hospital sounds drifted through the closed door — the squeak of shoes on linoleum, the distant beep of monitors, the low murmur of voices that never quite resolved into words. Not knowing how long I had, I prayed. I felt a presence in my dark room. I could not see anyone, but I could definitely feel someone was there. It was not a figure or a shape; it was simply a knowing, as certain as the bed beneath me. A warm feeling of peace filled the ward and my heart. I drifted in and out of sleep, acutely aware that the presence was still by my side. I must have dozed off and was awakened by small shafts of warm sunlight starting to filter through my hospital window, gently caressing my cheek. Morning. I was still here.

The ward door opened and a lovely, smiling lady came in to change my water carafe — and to her surprise, I did not have one. Nobody had thought to provide one. She busied herself dusting and then, as she was leaving, I heard a voice outside the door. "Has the South African woman died yet? I need her bed for another patient." The flustered registered nurse muttered something, and then I heard the lady who had just been in my ward say in broken English, "No, no — not dead. She not dead." The flustered nurse flew into the room, took one look at me, sighed, and did an immediate turnabout and promptly marched straight out again. The shift changed and fresh faces appeared.

It was not long before a very pretty, young doctor walked into my room. She was from North Africa. I immediately felt a kinship with her — fellow Africans, far from home. She smiled and came around to the side of my bed. "How are you feeling?" I said I had felt better in the past and forced a weary smile. She took my hand and said, "You do know that things are not looking promising right now, and we need to call your family."

I asked her what the time was and she said ten o'clock.

Immediately and without hesitation I said, "No, you can't call them — they are in church."

She gently stressed, "I don't think you understand. You are running out of time."

"No," I responded without hesitation. "I do not want you to call them, please. I need them there — they are praying for me." Her face changed. Her brow furrowed and she looked perplexed. She moved and sat on the side of my bed, still holding my hand. Her eyes were pleading, and I held my stance. Very determined. The logic of what I was saying made no sense to her, and I understood that. But there was a logic beyond medicine at work, and I trusted it more than I trusted the monitors and the charts.

She suddenly became very tearful. "Please," she whispered. "There isn't anything more I can do for you. I don't know how much longer you can hang on."

"They will come after church," I said. Unbeknown to me — and I would only find out once my husband arrived later — it was at that same moment that the whole church was praying for me. Ross had asked everyone to.

When he arrived later I was sitting up in bed, smiling. He stepped into the ward rather gingerly, as they had caught him in the corridor and given him the news. Unsure of what he would find, he most certainly was not expecting me to be sitting up with a huge smile on my face. The relief that swept over his face was visible. His whole body seemed to release a tension it had been holding since the corridor. His face broke out into the biggest smile. He went back to the door: "It's okay, Tammy — Mum is waiting for us. She is fine."

The following day a rather grumpy doctor arrived on her academic rounds with her students. She was obviously not a morning person, and definitely not a Monday morning person. She burst forth giving the students a rundown of my history, not once looking at me, as though I were a case study rather than a human being lying in the bed in front of her. She then pronounced that I would die of cancer. I was shocked. Where did she get that from?

As the students were leaving the room I called to her and asked her why she had said that. She was visibly irritated — how dare I question her. Her response was, "Well, if you don't die now, you will eventually die of cancer. People like you always do."

I looked straight at her. It took a great deal to restrain myself from saying exactly what came to mind at that moment. I said, "There is no conclusive evidence that I have cancer. I am still due to have the MRI scan."

"Well, you are dying anyway."

I shot straight back at her. I was not afraid of her. Doctors of various temperaments had been reporting to me for years. "Firstly, doctor, this is not the way you have been trained to speak to a patient. Secondly, only God decides when someone will die — and not you. God has decided I am not going to die, because if I was, it would have happened last night. Thirdly, I am not afraid of death. Something you do not seem very comfortable with yourself."

She gave me a piercing look and stormed out of the ward. I lay back against the pillows and let out a breath of exasperation. This would be the start of my journey, and eventually, months later, I would receive the diagnosis of Catastrophic Antiphospholipid Syndrome.

God walked every step of the way with me, opening doors and leading me to the correct medical team. Eventually, every doctor I saw gave me the same advice: go home — back to

South Africa. According to the medical team, it was time for me to say my goodbyes to family and friends.

Here I was at the end of 2012, lying in my sickbed in South Africa. All these questions floating in my head. The turquoise sea outside my window offered no answers, only its steady, indifferent beauty. I allowed my memories to transport me back to when I was seven years old.

Chapter One

Life Can Change in a Heartbeat

John 13:34: "A new command I give you: Love one another. As I have loved you, so you must love one another."

I was born and grew up in South Africa during the apartheid era. It was a strange time. The white English and Afrikaners despised each other, and both hated the black people, except for a group known as the white liberals, who were comprised of white South Africans. The divisions were not subtle. They were woven into every layer of daily life — into the schools, the buses, the park benches, the hospitals, the queues at the post office. As a child you did not understand the politics of it, but you understood the atmosphere. You understood the silence that fell when certain people walked into certain rooms, and you learned early which silences meant danger.

We were living in the mountains on a mine. I was seven years old at the time of this memory. I would imagine that I was like the Swiss character Heidi who lived in the mountains. Although not Swiss mountains, they too were beautiful, with green peaks. Goats and sheep would wander across the roads as they roamed freely. The mining village was located in a beautiful green valley at the foot of one of the many mountains around us. The village was self-contained. It had homes, a trading store, a hospital, a police station and a recreational club where the children would gather on weekends to watch movies. It offered every sport one could think of and included a huge swimming pool which was in use permanently in summer as we all frolicked and laughed in the summer sun. There was a pub where the adults would gather, and each evening as the golden African sun rolled down behind the mountain peak, leaving a blaze of red, orange and pink in the sky, this is when we would hear the harmonious singing of the African miners who lived a little further down in the valley in a compound. They would sing to the beating of African drums, a rhythm that would resound deep in my heart and eventually lull me to sleep. The only facilities missing were a school and a church. I would travel to school on a big yellow bus to a neighbouring mine that did have a school in its village. The mining village was a small, enclosed world with its own rhythms — the shift whistle in the morning, the rumble of the trucks on the gravel roads, the particular quiet that settled over the houses in the afternoon heat. The bus was driven by a kind and caring Indian driver who carefully and skillfully navigated the winding mountain road with precision. The school was co-ed and dual medium: English and Afrikaans. I had made friends with quite a few Afrikaans children, and we would play joyfully together in the big park in front of our house in the afternoons and on weekends. The strife of the adults did not affect us — or so it seemed. In the park, under the wide sky, we were simply children. The fact that the country around us was tearing itself apart along lines of colour and language had not yet reached us. Or so I believed.

One day my mum could not fetch me from the bus stop after school. She sent Miriam, our domestic worker, instead. Miriam had been with our family for as long as I could remember. She was a quiet, steady presence in our home, the kind of person who moved through her work with a grace that made it look effortless. As I disembarked from the bus and walked toward her, she gave me the warmest smile and a big hug. I was aware of someone behind me, and as I turned around, I saw my friends — the Afrikaans girls. I smiled at them, and they stared at me. The friendliness that had been there that morning had vanished, replaced by something cold and deliberate.

The one who had the most beautiful golden curls on her head and a real doll-like face stepped forward. Her dad was the local police constable. She was quite a ringleader — very bossy, the kind of child who set the tone for the group and expected the others to follow. She slowly started to chant the words "kafir boetie." Soon the other girls imitated her and they too started chanting "kafir boetie" — a derogatory Afrikaans phrase used for liberal individuals who accepted black people in South Africa. The chanting continued behind us, rhythmic and ugly, and Miriam hastily grabbed hold of my hand. Her grip was tight, almost painful, and I could feel a tremor running through her fingers. Out of the blue, a rock was hurled at her, hitting her on the head. Blood started oozing from under her white doek — a scarf she wore on her head. She started yelling and grabbed my hand tighter, and we started to run. There was a peal of laughter behind us, and then rocks and stones started hailing down on us. I could hear them striking the ground around our feet, bouncing off the road. By the time we got home, Miriam was sobbing uncontrollably. Her white doek was now a pale shade of blush pink. My mum had just returned home and watched on, horrified, as we ran up the driveway — Miriam howling, me in tow.

I explained the ordeal we had just encountered. My mum lifted Miriam's doek to inspect, and it was evident that she needed medical attention immediately. The gash on her head needed stitches. My mum got the big first aid box out of the cupboard and had Miriam sit down at the kitchen table whilst she wrapped a big bandage around her head and offered her a cup of sweet tea. Miriam sat there, her hands trembling around the cup, and I stood in the doorway watching, not fully understanding the weight of what had happened but understanding that the world I had known that morning was not the same world I had come home to. Mum then proceeded to phone my granny, who lived in the same mining village.

My grandpa — I called him Papa — and my granny arrived at six o'clock that evening, once my dad had returned from work. I was asked to relay the story of the events that had transpired that afternoon. I stood in the lounge and told it from beginning to end, aware of the way the adults' faces changed as I spoke. I was then ushered out of the room and told to play with my sister as the adults debated the events of the day.

My mother was crying. My dad was getting cross — that was his usual response when upset or stressed — telling her to pull herself together. Papa was silently listening and pondering the situation with a cup of tea in his hand, and Granny, very determined, had made up her mind. No grandchildren of hers would be subjected to such ill treatment. We would be sent to Vryheid, the town closest to us, to a multiracial, co-ed Roman Catholic boarding school. The decision was made that evening, and the speed of it left no room for argument. Within a week, we met the nuns and were enrolled in the Convent Primary School for the new school year starting in a few months' time.

My sister was five years old, and I was nearing my eighth birthday.

Chapter Two

A Little Miracle

Luke 18:16: "Let the little children come to me, and do not hinder them, for the kingdom of God belongs to such as these."

A few months after starting at the convent school, I woke up one morning with blood all over my pillow. The white cotton was stained a deep rust colour, and at first I could not understand where it had come from. I touched my face, my nose, my ears. I was so surprised and felt a little overwhelmed. The nuns were singing in chapel — I could hear the faint rise and fall of their voices through the walls — and Tembi, the lady who helped care for us, had not yet come up to the dorms. I crept out of my room and washed my pillowcase in the bathroom sink, scrubbing at the fabric until the water ran clear, and hid it behind my towel to dry.

This would become a morning ritual. I would wake up at five in the morning, when the nuns started singing, and sneak to the bathroom. The risks were high. If caught, the punishment was to be locked up in the "dark room" — a room used to store luggage, with no windows or ventilation, a cement floor, and shelves from floor to ceiling. A blanket and small stretcher were in the room. Anyone contravening any rule would be locked up there for the night. I wanted to avoid this punishment as much as I possibly could. The dark room was two doors down from my dorm, and I could hear the sobs emanating from it every night. The sound carried through the walls, thin and hopeless, and it conjured a great feeling of fear within me.

I noticed my gums had started bleeding, and I would wake up with blood all over my front teeth. When I brushed them, blood would ooze out of my gums, discolouring my white toothpaste and giving it a pink hue. I learned to brush gently, to rinse quickly, and to check my reflection before leaving the bathroom.

Bruises started to appear on my body. They arrived without explanation — I had not fallen, had not bumped into anything. They simply appeared, purple and tender, on my arms, my legs, my torso. It was almost July — winter holidays. I was due to go home. I counted the bruises one evening, lifting my pyjama sleeves in the dim dormitory light: twenty-three. How on earth was I going to explain all of this to my mum?

One morning whilst I was washing my pillowcase, Tembi suddenly appeared. It was much earlier than her usual time. Tembi — a sweet and direct twenty-two-year-old young Zulu woman — asked me what I was doing. I could not conjure a convincing excuse quickly enough, so I explained. She looked at the stained fabric in my hands, then at my face, and after a bit of negotiation she agreed not to tell anyone. Tembi would help me every morning to get rid of the evidence. She became my protective angel. When she went on her days off, Regina, a Zulu woman in her early thirties, would stand in. I managed to convince Regina to help me too. In return, I would teach her German in the suitcase room every Wednesday afternoon after homework. I had convinced her that it was not good for her not to know what the nuns were speaking about, just in case they were gossiping about her. I became a German tutor — my German was far from proficient, as I was still learning it myself — and she would make sure I had a clean, dry pillowcase on my bed every day. It was a fair arrangement, struck between a sick child and a kind woman, and it held.

It was eventually time to go on holiday. Thankfully, it was winter, and I wore my long-sleeved tops and jeans to hide my bruises. At home, I would sneak into the bathroom early in the morning to wash my pillowcase once my dad had left for work at five. One morning my mum caught me. She stood in the doorway and looked at the bloodied fabric in the sink, and then at me. Oh my word, the sky was falling! Out came the Reader's

Digest medical encyclopedia — the old version of Google. Within a few hours, both grannies knew I had a problem. My mother had already diagnosed me, or at least arrived at a suspicion grim enough to act upon, and I was duly shipped off to our general practitioner in Vryheid, the closest town.

He gave the disturbing news to my parents that I had leukaemia. I was not told I had leukaemia; I just knew that I was sick. Monitoring started with regular blood tests. Once I was back at school, I would take myself off to the doctor once a week. The nuns gave me permission to leave the property directly after school at two o'clock. I would walk the route alone, a small girl with a school bag over her shoulder and a purpose she could not fully explain to anyone.

On one of my walks to the doctor, I noticed a sign on a beautiful old red-brick building about two blocks from the school. The inscription on the building read: "The Child Welfare Society" — protecting children. This puzzled me, and I remember thinking: I wonder what that means. I did not yet have the vocabulary or the understanding to grasp the full weight of those words.

One day, my best friend at school confided in me that her stepfather was abusing her. She told me how he would abuse her every weekend when she went home. She hated nights, she said, as this is when he would creep into her bedroom. As she was explaining in great detail what he would do to her, I felt a wave of nausea, followed by total disgust and then panic and anguish. What was she talking about? My head was spinning. I did not understand. As she continued, I felt a slight tremble begin in my body. I remember staring at her in total bewilderment. This beautiful, caring girl sitting next to me was going through so much. Hearing her story made my illness pale into insignificance. My immediate reaction was: what can I do to help her? I was very much a person of action — and I still am to this day.

The story brought on a whole new dynamic within my own life. I began to fear my own dad. What if he made me do this? The fear was irrational, rooted in a child's inability to separate one man from another once the concept of danger had been introduced. No one explained the difference to me. No adult sat me down and drew a line between what my friend had suffered and what was normal. The silence around the subject allowed my confusion to harden into something that would take years to undo.

One day, whilst walking past the red-brick building on my way back from the doctor after having my regular blood tests done, I decided to pop in. A very kind Afrikaans lady was behind the desk. She had an unhurried, gentle manner that put me at ease. I explained my friend's dilemma, and the lady urged me to bring my friend in to see her. I went off with a skip in my step. Maybe I could help my friend.

I could not wait to tell her, and we came up with a plan on how we would get permission for her to leave the school grounds. My doctor visits had increased to twice a week, and I told the nun on duty that I was feeling a bit weak and asked if I could take my friend with me in case I felt worse. She agreed, so off the two of us set. We arrived at the red building, and I bounced in happily and introduced my friend to the kind Afrikaans lady. I explained that I was going to the doctor and I would return for my friend on my way back. I urged my friend to share everything she had told me. I had my blood tests done, and on my way back I collected my friend. The friendly lady squeezed my arm as we left, and my friend had a look of relief on her face that I had not seen before.

On our way back to the boarding, she told me that the lady had said that what her stepfather was doing to her was not normal, and no little girl should go through what she was going through. She had given the lady consent to phone her granny. A week later, my friend was moved to her granny's house for weekends and holidays. She and her little brother were safe at last.

She went to live with her biological father's parents — the most caring and amazing people. Slowly, she could start to heal from the trauma she had experienced. This event left a lasting impression on me and would affect my relationship with my own father forever, as no one explained it to me. I would be reluctant to hug or kiss him, and I would watch him like a hawk with my friends. My father loved giving hugs, and I resisted. So sad, as he was a gentle and kind soul who had done nothing to warrant my suspicion. The distance I created between us was born from a misunderstanding that nobody thought to address, and by the time I was old enough to understand it on my own, the habit had already taken root.

My illness continued to progress, and the doctors gave me three months to live. Blood would ooze from my ears too. My platelets plummeted, and our doctor referred me to a paediatrician. He was based in a big city, Pietermaritzburg, which was a four-hour drive away.

My health was deteriorating, and although no one spoke to me about it, I knew. Children are more perceptive than adults give them credit for. I could read the worry in my mother's face, the way conversations stopped when I entered a room, the too-bright cheerfulness in voices that were trying to hide something. My platelet count was decreasing significantly and rapidly. I had generalised pain in my body, especially in my legs. I would feel strange and very weak, and it felt like my blood was draining from my body. I would stand with my back against a cold wall just to feel the coldness run down my spine. It gave me the reassurance that if I could still feel the cold, I must still be alive. It was a small test I administered to myself each day, a private ritual of survival that no one else knew about.

I found a small empty shoebox. I had heard my grandparents speaking about a "will" to my parents. I took myself off to our school library and did some research on what it was, and I decided that I needed to write my own. I wrote a very rudimentary list of my belongings and who each item should go to. I put all my precious belongings into the shoebox — there were not many — and stapled names on each and left my "will" in the box. My Bible, bookmarks, a rosary, my bag of marbles... were a few of the items. I knew it would not be much longer. I could feel it. I knew I was dying. I was not afraid. I longed to meet Jesus, but I felt sad for my mum and dad. I did not want them to feel sad.

I was in the habit of going to the chapel each afternoon after homework. I loved the church — the smell of the polish on the pews, the smell of burning wax mingled with the smell of incense. These were scents that had become sacred to me, bound up with the feeling of safety and closeness to God. It lifted my spirits every time I pushed open the heavy wooden door and stepped inside.

One afternoon, the church was locked by the time I had finished homework at school. I wandered across the road back to the boarding, rather disappointed. I decided I would sneak upstairs to my room. We were not allowed upstairs at all — if caught, it would be punishment for me. But I was desperate to spend time with God: to tell Him of my day, to thank Him for all He was doing for me and my little sister, to thank Him for healing my body — I was totally convinced that He was — and to ask Him to continue. I would ask Him to help me be a witness among my friends.

That particular afternoon, I was in my dorm, kneeling in front of my bed on the cold, hard tile floor. I had a crucifix above my bed, and I was speaking to God and looking at the face of Jesus, who was looking down at me, when a bright light filled my room. It did not come from the window. It did not come from the passage. It was simply there, occupying the space around me with a warmth that had nothing to do with temperature. A sense of perfect peace came over me. I stayed very still. I did not want to disturb whatever was happening, as though any sudden movement might break the connection. When it passed, I finished my prayers and skipped downstairs with a lighter heart and a certainty that God was with me and all would be well.

I had to stay in boarding school that particular weekend and walked to the Anglican church with the other children from the boarding on Sunday morning to attend the service. After the service, I was outside getting ready to go back to school when the priest stopped all of us and asked if I could go back into the church with him. The other children looked at me with curiosity and mild concern. I followed him inside.

The church was dark, as all the lights had been turned off except for the little red light glowing above the tabernacle, signifying that the blessed host was present. We walked up the aisle. The beautiful stained-glass windows reflected a rainbow of colour across the room. The smell of snuffed candles lingered in the air. We knelt down in front of the altar at the communion rail. I cannot recall what the priest prayed, but I remember a warm feeling filling me from my head to my toes. It moved through me like water, gentle and thorough, reaching into places

I did not know were cold until they were warmed. I had the absolute certainty that I was healed. I totally believed it and could not contain myself.

As we walked out of the church, I looked up at the priest and told him that Jesus had healed me. His words still echo in my head to this day: "My child, we can have healing, even in death." I lamented, "No, no — I really am healed." He looked down at me with an expression I could not read at the time. Years later, I would understand it as the look of a man who wanted to believe a child but could not bring himself to, knowing what he knew. Unbeknown to me, my blood tests done on the Friday had returned dismal results. My platelet count was dangerously low. My mother had phoned the priest the night before to give him the news. Time was not on my side. My life was ebbing away.

When I returned to the boarding, I suddenly felt awful. I could not walk; pain was shooting in both legs, and I was carried to bed. I looked up at Jesus on the cross above my bed. I asked Him why. What had happened? Why was I in bed? I knew He had healed me that morning when the priest prayed for me. He was silent. That night my parents arrived. I said goodbye to my sister, who was very tearful that she was going to be left behind. The nun held her hand and promised her that she could sleep in her room. This became quite the topic for months to come — that my sister was able to see a nun's bedroom and a nun in her pyjamas!

As I was leaving, I told my sister about my shoebox in my cupboard and that if anything should happen to me, she could open it. Off we went, driving through the night. The headlights cut through the darkness, and I lay across the back seat, watching the stars through the window and listening to the low murmur of my parents' voices in the front. I would have an appointment with the paediatrician the next morning. He was a kind, efficient, and professional man.

As he was examining me on his consulting table, he spotted a necklace I had received from the Mother Superior when she visited the school a few weeks prior. She had come from Germany. The necklace was round, with a face of a cherub on the front, and at the back it was inscribed with the words "Gott ist lieb" — God is love.

He pointed at the pendant and asked me who gave it to me. I told him. He asked me what it meant in English, and I told him. He said, "Yvette, do you really believe that God loves you?" I remember saying, "Oh yes, I do," and he asked me why I believed that. Without hesitation I said, "Because God has healed me." He looked astonished and then puzzled. "But you are sick; that is why you are here. What makes you think He has healed you?" So I told him about the priest praying for me. He put his fingers on his chin and said, "Hmm... I see." He stood and stared at me, which felt like a very long time. He turned to my parents and said, "I think we need to do an urgent bone marrow biopsy to check what is going on."

I was sent off to the hospital down the road — St Anne's, a mission hospital. Off to theatre I went. The results came back very quickly. We found ourselves back in the paediatrician's consulting rooms. He looked at me and then he looked at my parents. "It appears that Yvette is quite right," the paediatrician explained. "Her bone marrow is reproducing platelets, and the lab technician said he could see them replicating as he was looking at the cells under the microscope."

A few days passed and there was a noticeable difference. I no longer felt weak and drained. The persistent bone aches had disappeared. The bleeding from my nose, mouth and ears had stopped. My platelet count was steadily climbing. It was not long before every symptom of illness had totally disappeared. I returned to the paediatrician. The team collected all my medical records and spent hours poring over them. There was no medical explanation for the unexplained changes in my body.

Yes, my bone marrow was responding and it continued to generate platelets. The unanswered question was: how? How could this be? What had prompted this unexpected change?

It was a miracle — an answer to prayer. So many people had prayed for me every day, and God had heard their prayers. From that day on, I thought that miracles happened to everyone. I believed totally, and still do, that if you pray, God hears you and heals you.

We will never know why certain events happen in our lives, but what I do know is that my faith grew exponentially from that moment. God used a challenging time to touch others. I may have experienced a traumatic event which resulted in me being sent to boarding school; however, if I had not gone to boarding school, I would not have been close to my doctor. I would not have been able to help my friend. The people who prayed for me would never have got to experience the joy of answered prayer and God's miracles.

Chapter Three

The Nest

Psalm 27:1: "The Lord is my light and my salvation; whom shall I fear? The Lord is the stronghold of my life; of whom shall I be afraid?"

2012 — Here I was once again back in South Africa, lying in a sickbed. Clots were coursing through my body, affecting every organ. Medication was not helping. The days blurred together, each one a repetition of the last: pain, medication, rest, and the steady hum of a body that refused to cooperate with the treatment being poured into it. I prayed, and I heard my answer. It was like a quiet whisper in my mind — not a voice I heard with my ears, but a knowing that arrived with a clarity I could not have manufactured on my own.

When I was eight years old, I had trusted God totally. There was no fear. My faith had been simple and absolute, the faith of a child who had never learned to doubt. Now I had allowed fear to creep into my thoughts. It had arrived gradually, carried in on the back of medical reports and the measured voices of specialists and the worried expressions of people who loved me. God showed me that this was a barrier between myself and Him — a barrier to my healing. What a revelation that was to me. It had not even crossed my mind. Fear had become so familiar, so constant a companion, that I had stopped recognizing it as something separate from myself. I confessed immediately and repented of my sin.

Later on the same day, I was reading and praying silently when a thought came into my head. The words "The Nest" stuck. They arrived without context or explanation — just two words that planted themselves in my mind and refused to be dislodged. I was not sure what this meant. I prayed again, and the words seemed louder, more insistent. My husband, Ross, walked into the room, and I said to him, "I think God wants us to go to The Nest, but I don't understand why."

The only Nest we knew of was a resort in the Drakensberg, a well-known mountain range in South Africa. He looked at me and said, "Why don't you ask God again?" My daughter, Tammy, walked in at that moment and said, "Mum, have you Googled it?" I had not. "Well, Google and see what comes up." I lifted my phone and did just as Tammy suggested. The first item that popped up was a link to "The Nest," a homeless shelter in our city. I was puzzled. I had never been to a homeless shelter before. I had driven past people living on the streets, of course, but the world they inhabited was entirely unknown to me. When Ross came in, I told him it was a homeless shelter and not a resort. He said, "Pray and ask God if that is the one." I did, and it still came back strongly that it was.

I filled in the electronic form stating that I would like to visit, pressed the send button, and then I prayed, "Lord, if you would like me to visit The Nest, I am trusting that you are healing me. Here I am, Lord — use me as an instrument to share your love." From that moment on, all fear had left me. My focus was on getting better. It was as though the act of committing to something beyond my own illness had loosened its grip on me. I had given God my fear and received a purpose in return.

Three months went by, and I had not heard from The Nest; however, I was getting stronger. The improvement was gradual, measured not in dramatic leaps but in small victories that would have been invisible to anyone watching from the outside. I was able to get out of bed and walk to the bathroom myself. I practised walking down the upstairs passage leading off my bedroom, one hand on the wall, counting my steps. Eventually, I was strong enough to walk down the staircase. The first day I was able to walk down, I was standing in the living room, rather delighted with conquering the feat, when my phone rang. A male voice on the other side of the phone said, "Good morning, my name is Soswa from The Nest. We have received your email. When would you like to come and visit?"

Now, if that is not a sign, what is!

God had blessed me with healing, and now I was able to visit The Nest. I spoke to Ross, and we agreed that as soon as I was able to walk down the driveway to the garden gate, he would take me. The Nest was in a very dangerous area of the city of Durban, South Africa. Ross made a joke and said I would need to put running shoes on when we visited, in case I needed a fast getaway. I laughed, and it felt good to laugh. It had been a long time since laughter had come easily.

The day arrived. I was ready to visit The Nest. We made the call and arranged a day and time. On my arrival at The Nest, we stood at the door. My heart sank. There was a flight of stairs. I would count the stairs at a later stage — there were fifty-two. How was I possibly going to get up there? My legs, which had only recently remembered how to carry me across a room, were being asked to climb a small mountain. Ross was very positive. "We will do it slowly, one step at a time. It doesn't matter how long it takes you. There is no rush."

We started our great ascent, Ross helping me, his arm steady beneath mine. I was exhausted and elated when I eventually arrived at the top landing, breathing hard but upright. We were met by a friendly young man, Jacques, who was the pastor of the little church at the top of the stairs to the right. Soswa was not there, but Jacques would be taking us around. We started with the room where he hosted a church. It was a modest space, with plastic chairs arranged in rows and a small wooden lectern at the front. We then went down the passage and popped our heads into the living room. There were a few residents sitting, smoking, and watching television. They glanced up at us with the brief, practised appraisal of people who had learned to size up strangers quickly. They had a small dining area and a kitchen enclosed behind bars. A large, cheerful lady was cooking the evening dinner of boiled cabbage and pap — a stiff maize porridge. She waved and shouted a warm welcome that carried down the corridor and seemed to soften the whole building.

We then entered the sleeping quarters. I had never been in a shelter. I had no idea what to expect, but nothing could have prepared me for what I saw. The room was huge — a large warehouse filled with one hundred and twenty bunk beds. It was dark, and Jacques explained that electricity charges are high, so they only turn the lights on at night. Men and women shared the same area. It came as a shock to me. I am a very private person, and seeing the lack of privacy felt like I had been kicked in the stomach by a horse. It really affected me. I felt nauseous. I could not conceal how shocked I was. I tried to hide my feelings by forcing a smile and a nod. Ross whispered, "Are you alright?" I nodded a yes, though I was far from alright. I was trying to reconcile the world I came from — the private hospitals, the corner offices, the controlled environments of my professional life — with the reality of what was in front of me. Jacques continued the tour. There were only two toilets and two showers for the men, and two showers and two toilets for the women. For one hundred and twenty people. What an awakening it was for me. I could not believe what I was seeing.

I asked Jacques what the needs were. This would be the start of a five-year relationship with The Nest. I first started by helping with collections of food donations. Then I assisted the management to register as a non-profit organization, as it was privately owned and not subsidized by the government or any other organization. I did all the paperwork and submitted the application. Slowly, I ventured into the dormitory. I started to forge relationships with the residents, learning their names, hearing their stories, understanding that behind every face was a life as complex and layered as my own. I would eventually start counselling residents twice a week. I then started a Bible study once a week. I was amazed at the positive response. People who had been cast aside by the world were hungry for something that told them they still mattered.

There were elderly permanent residents, and they were the people who attended on a regular basis. I then started involving church groups and corporate organizations to raise funds. It would be a time of learning for me — getting to know more about the life of the homeless, how they survived, and what their daily challenges were. People do not choose to be homeless. Life, unfortunately, dishes out a bad hand. Not all were dependent on drugs, although I did get to know drug addicts and drug dealers. I was threatened by dealers not to convert their clientele to Christianity, and they warned that if I did, they would come after me, as that was their bread and butter. Converts would no longer want to buy drugs. I heard the threat and carried on regardless. I had not survived everything I had survived to be frightened by men who sold poison on street corners.

I befriended the prostitutes. It was an interesting mindset to learn about. Some had been forced into prostitution as very young girls and did not know any other way of life. Some found themselves having to fend for themselves, had nowhere else to turn, and fell into prostitution. They saw it as a job and would speak about going to work. There was no shame in the way they described it, only a practical acceptance of the hand they had been dealt.

A lot of the homeless turned to begging, each having their own "place of work" at specific traffic lights. They respected each other's territory and did not venture into the other's "office space," as they would refer to it. There was an order to it, an unwritten system of rules that governed their days as surely as any employment contract.

They all worked out the system of how to obtain food. Different churches and organizations offered soup kitchens on different days. If they knew where to go, they were able to get a meal every day. The shelter provided a bowl of porridge in the morning and a rudimentary evening meal. Residents had to pay for a cup of tea or coffee. They also paid for their washing to be done and, of course, their rent. Everything cost something, even at the very bottom.

Those who were not living in shelters but on pavements had no access to running water or a place to shower or wash their clothing. So often we complain that they smell dreadful, but do we ever take time to consider their dilemma? I was upset once when I saw a homeless person throw clothing into a bin. I marched up to him and asked him why he was doing that. It had never occurred to me that they could not wash their clothing. They would wear the clothes until they could no longer stand the smell themselves, and then change into clean, oversized clothing they would receive as a donation. The old garments were simply discarded, because there was no alternative. It was a small detail that rearranged something in my understanding of the world, and I have never looked at a person in dirty clothing the same way since.

I was stunned by how many people had lost good careers — so many with degrees. Was this endemic to the political situation in the country? A country where unemployment ran high. Poverty spread like a virus, and white men were no longer given job opportunities due to the new BBBEE targets, which required black men to be employed instead. Alcoholism had gripped so many. It offered an escape from the humiliation and pain of loss. Drugs seemed to circulate freely. A drug syndicate ran the streets.

A few years after I started volunteering at The Nest, my husband and I were watching a documentary on drug cartels. The house was quiet, the evening had settled in, and we had the television to ourselves. I slipped off to the kitchen to make us each a cup of tea. As I walked back into the sitting room, there was a Nigerian man on the television. I was so excited. I said to Ross, "Oh look, there's my friend, Tokyo."

He looked totally aghast at me and said, "What do you mean he is your friend?"

Unbeknown to me, the tall, well-built black man with chains of gold hanging around his neck and gold teeth was the kingpin of drug dealing — the main drug lord of the area I volunteered in. I had spoken with him many times at The Nest, shared pleasantries, even accepted his help carrying donated goods inside. He had always been polite, even cordial. I had no idea who he really was, or what world he inhabited once he walked through the shelter's front door and out into the streets. This is how God protected my every encounter. I went about my God-given business, and no one tried to stop me or harm me. God once again showed me His omniscience and omnipresence.

Chapter Four

A Bird with a Broken Wing

Ephesians 3:19: "...and to know this love that surpasses knowledge, that you may be filled to the measure of all the fullness of God."

I was a bird with a broken wing. I felt I fitted in perfectly. The residents were all broken too. There was no pretence required inside the walls of The Nest, no performance to maintain. The world outside the shelter demanded that you present a version of yourself that was polished and acceptable. Inside, no such effort was necessary. They all accepted me for who I was — no questions asked. I, in turn, embraced all of the residents. I listened to their stories, their sorrows and their joys. Some spoke in fragments, revealing only as much as they could bear in a single sitting. Others poured out decades of hurt as though the dam had finally broken and they needed a witness to the flood.

They taught me to love unconditionally, not to judge them. They did not judge each other. There was an unspoken code among the residents: whatever your past held, whatever had brought you through those doors, it did not define how you were treated inside. They were kind to me, and in return, I did my best to help each of them when they approached me for help. I did not see them as people who needed to be rescued. I just wanted to love them the way they loved me. There is a particular honesty that lives among people who have lost everything. When the trappings of status and wealth are stripped away, what remains is raw and unguarded. I found that honesty both humbling and refreshing.

Having an autoimmune condition can be rather challenging, as my immune system was severely compromised. The environment has a big impact on my wellbeing. I had worked in the hospital environment for thirty years, and now I could not set foot into a hospital without acquiring some virus. The sterile corridors that had once been so familiar to me had become hostile territory for my weakened defences.

1989 — I was reminded of a time when I was a trainee nurse. Even though my immune system was often compromised, I would push through. I was always chosen to "special" very sick and often contagious cases. It never entered my head that I could decline based on my immune condition. I would never make an excuse. I saw this as my duty to serve God by taking care of my patients. It was not bravery. It was simply what I believed I was there to do.

I was assigned to a month's night duty, and when I reported on duty I was told I would be "specialing" a young twenty-eight-year-old man who had been travelling around the country with a circus. He originally came from North Africa. I knew nothing more about him than that.

I was required to double gown, wear a cap and mask, double glove, and wear extra theatre boots over my shoes as covers. We did not have hazmat suits in those days. I was not permitted to be in contact with anyone else whilst I was nursing him. I would be relieved by another trainee nurse. We both were given large "rugby ball" shape capsules to take each day as a prophylactic. The tablets gave our urine a distinct red colour. The patient was nursed in an oxygen tent. He was so frightened. He could not speak English and could not understand me. We communicated in the only language available to us: gestures, touch, and the tone of a voice even when the words meant nothing. I would speak to him softly, hoping that the sound itself offered some comfort, even if the meaning was lost. Blood oozed from him. He was bleeding internally and externally. Slowly his organs began to shut down, and I watched it happen with the helplessness of someone holding a hand they cannot save.

At first I was not aware of his diagnosis. When the results came back confirming that he had Ebola, there was quite a stir in the corridor. Voices dropped to urgent whispers. The atmosphere on the ward shifted. Someone asked me at the door if I was sure I wanted to nurse him. It would only be a few weeks later that I discovered that everyone had refused to nurse him, as they were afraid — except for myself and the nurse who relieved me. I remember thinking: well, if I don't, who will? At that stage I did not realise that I had an autoimmune condition and how compromised my body was, and yet God protected me. I chose to serve my patient unconditionally because I asked myself: what would Jesus do in this situation? The answer was never complicated.

My patient died a few nights into my shift. I was devastated at the loss of such a young life to such a dreadful disease. It was a traumatic death for me to witness. The oxygen tent could not contain the reality of what was happening inside it. Not once did I doubt that God had His hand of protection over me. Not once did I allow any negative thought of: what if I contracted Ebola?

My approach to The Nest was exactly the same. I believed wholeheartedly in God's protection over me.

This brings me back to The Nest. One would think that working in a shelter riddled with bed bugs, rats, tuberculosis, and HIV would yield a negative immune response, but it did not. The irony was not lost on me. A hospital, designed to heal, made me ill. A shelter, where disease lurked in every corner, left me untouched. Strangely, I never picked up any virus from the shelters in the five years that I was involved with them. I have always believed that as God sent me there, He protected me and my immune system.

Whilst volunteering in the shelter, I started a knitting group to make articles for the residents to sell. The money would go toward their individual rental at the shelter. Yarn had become a fashionable material to use for a craft, and I saw an opportunity in it. I had been a businesswoman all my life. I did not know the first thing about crafts. My hands were more accustomed to spreadsheets and business proposals than to needles and skeins of wool. But I was up to the challenge. Thank goodness for YouTube!

I would spend time with the ladies learning together to crochet yarn items: bathmats, holders, bags, and more. The early attempts were comical. Lopsided squares that were meant to be rectangles. Bags with holes large enough to lose their contents through. We laughed at ourselves freely and without embarrassment. Slowly, though, our fingers learned the rhythm of the hook and yarn, and what had started as clumsy effort began to take shape as something worth selling. Eventually, once we had perfected the art of yarn work, I reserved a table once a month at a market.

I would collect the ladies from the shelter along with their goods, and take them to the market. They were so sweet. On market days the atmosphere in the shelter shifted. The ladies would dress beautifully in donated clothing, carefully chosen and pressed the night before. They applied makeup with the concentration of artists preparing for an exhibition. Hair was styled, shoes were polished, and there was a lightness in their step that was absent on ordinary days. They loved the experience. It was not only about selling. It was because they felt part of the local community. No one at the market knew that they were homeless. They were like everyone else, swapping stories with other vendors, having a laugh and a cup of tea with members of the community. For those few hours they were not defined by their circumstances. They were simply women with something to offer, and the community received them as such. It became the highlight of their month, and I confess it became the highlight of mine too.

God was teaching me to listen to Him, to follow His direction every day, even when I did not feel like going to The Nest. I was beginning to understand that obedience is not always accompanied by enthusiasm. Sometimes it is simply a matter of showing up, trusting that He will use you once you arrive.

Chapter Five

The Story of Divan

Luke 12:7: "Indeed, the very hairs of your head are all counted. Do not be afraid; you are worth more than many sparrows."

2014 — One day after working at school — I had bought a school which helped me fund my work with the homeless — I was standing in my kitchen. The afternoon light came through the windows and fell across the counter in long amber stripes. I felt so sick and very tired. The kind of tiredness that settles into your bones and makes even the simplest task feel monumental. I decided to make a cup of tea, hoping it might revive me. I was supposed to go to The Nest that afternoon, and I really did not feel like it.

As the kettle was boiling, I was having an internal tussle about going. I told God I would go "another day." Surely one afternoon off would make no difference. The shelter would carry on without me. The residents would hardly notice my absence. The answer came back very clearly: Go now! It was not a voice I heard with my ears, but a command that reverberated through my entire being with an authority I could not ignore. I was stubborn. I said no and proceeded to make my cup of tea.

As I took a sip, the urge was so strong that I had to go to The Nest. It built in my chest like a pressure that would not release. I banged my cup down on the kitchen counter saying, "Well, fine then!"

I marched to the key drawer, took the car keys out, and locked the kitchen door. I was a very unhappy person. As I drove along, I really complained. I don't feel well. Why do I have to go today? I am sure they can manage for one day without me. The streets rolled past the window and I grumbled the entire way, a reluctant servant being dragged to her post.

I arrived at The Nest. It had just gone one o'clock in the afternoon. The heat of the day pressed down on the building. I climbed the stairs. The mural of the angel at the top of the stairs was looking down at me. The words inscribed on the wall were "Come to me, all you who are heavy laden, and I will give you rest." (Matthew 11:28) They were barely visible, as over time they had faded, the paint cracking and peeling at the edges. I had passed that mural dozens of times, but that afternoon the words seemed to hang in the air with particular weight.

I stepped onto the landing. Everything was unusually silent — not one voice was to be heard. The Nest was never silent. There was always a conversation somewhere, a radio playing, an argument brewing or resolving. I stuck my head into the sitting room, and it was strangely empty. The usual smokers were not sitting having their afternoon puff. The plastic chairs that normally held three or four people at any given moment sat vacant, as though everyone had been called away at once. I strode through to the dorm, and very few were asleep on their beds. The dorm was quite deserted. I walked back into the connecting passage. "Well, I am here. What do you want me to do, Lord?" I was puzzled. I stood in the corridor and waited, as though expecting an answer to materialise from the peeling walls.

A man scuttled past me. I had never seen him before. He was wearing a big black overcoat, which seemed out of place in the afternoon heat, and he descended the flight of stairs quickly, his head bowed. I was still trying to fathom out why the Lord wanted me there when I suddenly got the notion that I should speak to the man who had just walked past me. It was a thought that arrived fully formed and insistent. I rushed to the top of the stairs just as he reached the bottom, and he was about to step out the door.

I called out, "Excuse me, excuse me!"

He stopped and looked up at me. His face was drawn, his eyes shadowed with a weariness that went beyond fatigue.

I was not sure what to say next. I had to think quickly. "You don't know me. My name is Yvette. I visit here from time to time."

He looked bewildered. "I haven't met you. What is your name?"

"Divan," he replied. His voice was flat, colourless.

"Hi Divan. Do you have a short moment to chat?"

He blinked and hesitated. "What do you want to talk about?"

I felt awkward. What would I say to him? I had no prepared speech, no pamphlet to hand over. I was a woman standing at the top of a staircase with nothing but a feeling that she was supposed to be there.

"I would like to get to know you a little, if you have time."

He hesitantly started back up the stairs and met me halfway. I asked him if we could sit down. We sat on the steps, the concrete cool beneath us.

I asked him a bit about himself. He was surprisingly open, as though he had been carrying the weight of his story for so long that the mere invitation to speak was enough to loosen its hold. He told me he was an alcoholic, which had caused him to lose his wife and family and eventually his job. He spoke about his children with a tenderness that made it clear how much their absence pained him. He described how one loss had led to another, each one compounding the last, until the life he had once known was unrecognisable. He did not know how he would be able to get over his loss.

We chatted about this for some time. I spoke to him, encouraging him and reminding him that the Lord loves him and wants the best for him. I felt totally inept and out of my comfort zone. The words coming from my mouth felt insufficient against the enormity of his pain. Who stops a strange man and just strikes up an arbitrary conversation with him? And yet here I was, sitting on a concrete step in a homeless shelter, talking to a man I had never met, because a voice inside me had insisted I could not stay home.

Eventually, Divan asked me if I would go into the dorm with him to his bunk bed, as he wanted to show me something. I was not sure about his request — it made me feel unsettled — but I felt I needed to display confidence. After all, the Lord had brought me there that day. We walked through the quiet dorm, past rows of empty bunks, until we reached his. He asked me to sit on his bed. The mattress was thin and sagged in the middle.

Then he pulled a rope from the black backpack he was carrying. It had a noose tied at one end. The fibres were rough and tightly wound. He had prepared it carefully. He burst into tears. As the tears streamed down his face, he confessed that he could not see any way forward in his life and was heading to a nearby bridge. He intended to tie the rope to the bridge and then jump off. The black overcoat, I realised, had been chosen to conceal what he carried.

I asked him what had changed his mind, and he told me that when I said Jesus knows him and loves him, he felt he wanted to get to know Jesus more. Something in those simple words had reached through the fog of his despair and offered him a thread to hold on to. There and then, we prayed together and he gave his life to the Lord. We sat on that bunk bed, two strangers brought together by a force neither of us fully understood in the moment, and we prayed.

What a huge lesson I learned that day. Firstly, not to argue with God when He asks me to do something. Secondly, life is not all about how I am feeling. Thirdly, it is important to be obedient to God. My tiredness and reluctance that afternoon could have cost a man his life. The thought of that has never left me.

What happened to Divan? He eventually got a job, found love, and moved into an apartment. If I had not obeyed God that day, he would have died. God loves each of us. He knows our circumstances, and He wants to protect us.

You may be asking: how do you hear God?

It is sometimes a very strong, urgent feeling. It can be a thought that just will not leave me, no matter how I try to push it aside. It may be through a verse in the Bible that suddenly leaps from the page with fresh meaning. Whatever it is, I usually know it is from God because, firstly, it is not a thought or action I would voluntarily think of on my own. Secondly, there is an urgency that starts to build up inside of me, a restlessness that does not subside until I act. It is uncomfortable, and I have learned that the discomfort is the point. God does not wait for us to be comfortable before He calls us to move.

Chapter Six

A Protective Hand

Psalm 121:7–8: "The Lord will keep you from all harm — he will watch over your life; the Lord will watch over your coming and going both now and forevermore."

1989 — Divan's story reminded me of a situation I found myself in when I was doing my second year of nurse training. I had just finished a stint of seven twelve-hour shifts on day duty. It was Friday, and I could not wait to end my shift at seven o'clock that evening. I had planned to have dinner, soak in a tub filled with bubble bath, put my pyjamas on, and watch a good movie with a big bowl of popcorn sprinkled with salt and vinegar. The kind of evening that exists only in your imagination during a long week, growing more perfect with each passing hour. Plans set, I ran from the ward to the dining room, happy to put the week behind me.

I was just putting the final fork of fish into my mouth when the dining room phone rang. One of my colleagues answered it and called me. I gulped down my last mouthful of juice and went to the phone. As I answered the call, I heard sobbing on the other side. It took a few seconds to work out who was speaking to me. It turned out to be a girlfriend of a patient I had nursed on the medical ward. Eventually I managed to calm her down, and she explained she did not know who to turn to and thought I might be able to help her, so she phoned the hospital reception, who transferred her call.

Through her sobs she told me her boyfriend, Ricardo, had threatened to take his own life. He was with her in her apartment and she did not know what she should do. Her voice kept breaking, and I could hear in the gaps between her words the particular panic of someone who has exhausted every option they can think of and has arrived at the last one. I agreed to go across immediately. Not knowing what I would find, I asked a male cousin of mine to meet me outside her apartment. I had never dealt with anything of this nature before. My training had covered wound care and medication administration and the mechanics of keeping a body alive. It had not covered this.

We both went into the apartment. Liz met us at the door. Her eyes were puffy, swollen and red from crying. Her hands were shaking. I told her to wait in the kitchen and went through to the sitting room where Ricardo was. My cousin, Gary, was right behind me. What was awaiting me came as a total shock. There was Ricardo standing in the middle of the sitting room, holding a gun to his temple. The room was very still. I signalled to Gary to stop, as Ricardo did not know him.

I started speaking in a gentle tone, and Ricardo was not interested. He started to shout at me. This was not working out as I had seen in the movies. I was so tired from my long shift, and suddenly, I do not know what came over me, but I got so mad with Ricardo. I shouted back, telling him he was the most selfish individual I had ever met, and if he was going to do something, to do it outside on the lawn so that we were not expected to clear up his mess. I was shaking, I was so cross. My face went puce and my already big eyes widened even more. It was not a strategy. It was not a technique. It was exhaustion and frustration overriding every instinct I had.

Then Ricardo did something I had hoped for but did not expect — he put the gun down. The metal made a dull sound against the table. Gary was fuming with me. I looked at Ricardo and said, "Well, I am glad we have reached an understanding!" I took the gun away and marched out of the house. My mind was reeling. What was I to do next?

Gary was waiting at the car. He started yelling at me. "Are you stupid? He could have pulled the trigger and killed not only himself but us as well. I am going home!" He drove off. I stood in the car park, suddenly aware of the quiet and of the fact that I was entirely alone with a situation that was far from resolved. Then I became aware of Ricardo standing behind me. I told him to get into my car — I would drop him off at home.

As we neared his apartment building he said, "I don't want to be alone." The words were quiet, stripped of all the earlier bravado and rage. I looked at him. What was I to do with this man? I hardly knew him, and I could not take him to the nurses' home. The first thing that came to mind was to take him to my dad.

I told him to get out of the car, pack his bag, phone Liz and tell her that I was taking him to my dad, who is a priest, and I would be back for him. It was already half past eight in the evening. I knew if I called my mother she would not be happy that I was driving my little VW Beetle at night. It was a good two-hour drive to their home. I had only had my driver's licence for a few months. I phoned, and thankfully my dad answered. I told him that I had a difficult situation and needed his help with a friend, and I would explain everything once I arrived.

I then set off to fetch Ricardo. He was waiting outside with a small bag. He got into my Beetle and off we went. My driving skills were horrendous. My car lights were quite dim, and it was difficult to see the dark highway. Those days the roads were not lit up as they are now. My one car light shone a few metres ahead but the other shone into the bush alongside the road like a spotlight. We bumped and ground along. I decided to follow the coastal road. I noticed Ricardo became very quiet, and his focus was on the road. Every now and again he would warn me that we were getting too close to the edge. We were following a coastal road which was quite narrow. Sugarcane flanked one side of the road, but the side we were driving on had a sheer cliff dropping away into darkness. Ricardo looked exceptionally nervous.

We eventually arrived, and my dad came outside to meet us. The porch light was on, and he stood in the doorway in his dressing gown with the calm of a man who had been woken by emergencies before. I had hidden the gun under my seat. I handed it to my dad and said I would explain in the morning. When I turned around to see where Ricardo was, he was on his knees kissing the ground.

My dad said, "Son, are you alright?"

Ricardo looked up at him. "Sir, I have never been so frightened in all my life. My life flashed before me. Your daughter's driving is so scary I thought I was going to die!"

My dad laughed.

"No, really, sir, it's no joke — and I realised I am not ready to die!"

My driving may have made Ricardo realise that he was not ready for death just yet. The entire experience, on the other hand, made me realise how many people in our world are hurting and do not know who to turn to. There is a loneliness that comes before desperation, and it is often invisible to the people standing closest. This is what prompted me to train in psychology, and when I met Divan I thankfully no longer had to rely on what I had seen in a movie — I was able to apply what I had been trained to do.

Was God there that night? He was. He was protecting all of us from my ignorance and stupidity, convicting Ricardo too. Ricardo and Liz became good friends of mine. Ricardo lived for a further six years and then passed away in a devastating car accident.

Chapter Seven

Reggie

Exodus 33:17: "I know you by name."

2015 — On my many visits to The Nest, I noticed a short man with a friendly face and inquiring blue eyes. He had a tracheotomy in situ in his throat and struggled to speak. When he tried, the sound that emerged was a raspy whisper that most people found too difficult to decipher. Rather than withdraw into silence, he had found another way. He would walk around with a small blackboard and a piece of chalk, scribbling messages and holding the board up with a grin, as though he were a street performer inviting you into his act. We started to chat — him writing, me reading aloud, both of us laughing at the peculiar rhythm of our exchanges. I discovered that his name was Reggie.

Reggie had an amazing sense of humour. Even through the limitations of chalk and blackboard, his wit was sharp and quick. He had been a sailor most of his life and had tales of the sea and faraway lands. He would describe ports he had visited with such colour and detail that I could almost smell the salt air and hear the creak of the ship beneath his feet. He told me about storms that had rattled the hull, about sunrises seen from the deck that he said no photograph could ever capture. The sea had been his whole world, and he spoke of it the way some men speak of a first love — with reverence and a quiet ache for something that could not be recovered.

One evening, I noticed that Reggie was not in his bed. His blackboard sat on his pillow, the chalk resting neatly beside it. Three days passed, and Reggie was not around. No one seemed particularly concerned. In a shelter, people came and went. Absence was not unusual. But Reggie's empty bunk unsettled me. I eventually asked his neighbour in the bunk next to Reggie's. He told me that Reggie had been taken away in an ambulance some days earlier. He did not know much more than that.

I asked the manager of the shelter if he knew which hospital Reggie had been taken to, and he did not know. So often in shelters, people are totally forgotten. One becomes a faceless being. As long as the rent is paid, no one cares. There are no next-of-kin details on file, no emergency contacts, no one to call or be called. A person can simply vanish, and the space they occupied is filled by someone new before the mattress has cooled. I felt a sudden, inexplicable urge within me to find

Reggie. It was the same insistent pull I had felt before, the one I had learned not to ignore.

I phoned my husband, Ross, and he agreed to meet me at the shelter after he had finished work. When he arrived early that evening, still in his work clothes, I asked him if he would accompany me to the hospital to find Reggie. Durban is a big city. It would be like searching for a needle in a haystack. But Ross did not hesitate. He could see the determination on my face and he trusted it, even when the logic of the situation suggested we were unlikely to succeed.

We went to the hospital where the shelter folk were usually admitted. We gave them Reggie's name and what little description we could offer: short, blue eyes, tracheotomy. The staff checked their records and came back shaking their heads. No Reggie. We thanked them and set off to another government hospital across the city.

When we arrived at this particular hospital, it felt as though we were stepping back into the dark ages. The building itself seemed to groan under the weight of years of underfunding and neglect. It had dark, oppressive walls stained with damp. Pipes with steam puffing out from them ran along the ends of dark passages, and the air carried the sharp smell of disinfectant that could not quite mask what lay beneath it. The corridors were generally very unkempt, with peeling linoleum underfoot and flickering fluorescent lights that cast everything in a sickly pallor. We searched the wards. We asked at the nurses' stations. We could not find Reggie.

We truly had no idea where to look next. Ross and I were at a loss. There are numerous hospitals in Durban. Where should we go next? We prayed when we got back to the car. We sat in silence, and Ross eventually asked me where we should try next. It was getting late — well past visiting hours — and it would be difficult to enter any hospital after eight at night. Suddenly a hospital came to mind. One I had not thought of in many years and had never been to. Only the Lord could have given me that thought. We decided to give it a try. It was a mission hospital on the outskirts of the city. It was midnight. We had been on the hunt for Reggie since six that evening, driving from one end of Durban to another, speaking to night staff who were tired and understandably confused by two strangers asking about a man they could barely describe.

At last, we found him. The night superintendent was not too happy to let us in. She stood in the doorway of the ward, arms folded, her expression making it clear that midnight visitors were not welcome. After much persuasion — and I suspect she relented more to be rid of us than out of sympathy — she gave us a few minutes.

We took the lift up to Reggie's ward. I had no idea what was wrong with him or if he would even recognise us. The ward was dim, the only light coming from the nurses' station at the far end. We walked past rows of sleeping patients until we reached his bed. There he was — his big blue eyes beaming as he saw me approach. Despite everything, that smile was unmistakable. He had suffered a stroke. One side of his body lay still, but his eyes were alive with recognition. His sense of humour was still very much intact. He knew us instantly, and we were able to have a chat with him. I told him how worried we had been and how much he was loved. He could not write on his blackboard — his writing hand was affected — but he nodded and his eyes said what his chalk could not.

The name above his bed read: "John Doe."

That simple, anonymous label broke something inside me. This man who had sailed the world, who had made me laugh with his blackboard jokes, who had lived a full and varied life, had been reduced to two words that meant nobody. We were able to give the staff his identification number and details about him. They were so grateful. Their John Doe now had a name and a past. A history. A person.

We left the hospital feeling a sense of relief. We once again sat in our car and thanked the Lord. At least some dignity was restored to Reggie. A few days later I popped in to see him again. He had suffered another stroke and did not recognise me at all. His blue eyes looked through me as though I were a stranger, and perhaps in his mind I was. I left with a heavy heart, but I was also so grateful that God had given me the opportunity to see him before, and that we had been able to speak to him. He knew he was loved and that someone cared.

I would receive a call at three in the morning, two days later, from the hospital, to tell me that Reggie had passed away peacefully. I put the phone down and sat in the dark of our bedroom for a long while. I was grateful that in his final days, Reggie had been known. That the staff who cared for him could call him by his name.

I was reminded that every person is special in the Lord's eyes. Not one of us is forgotten. He knows where we are and what we are going through. God placed it on my heart to find Reggie so that his dignity could be restored. He was not a John

Doe. He was Reggie. God knows each of us by name, and He wants us to know that He knows us and cares for us.

Isaiah 43:1: "I have called you by name; you are mine."

Reggie will forever live in my heart.

Chapter Eight

Voices

Isaiah 41:10: "Do not fear, for I am with you; do not be dismayed, for I am your God. I will strengthen you and help you; I will uphold you with my righteous right hand."

2016 — I had arrived at The Nest one afternoon with a big food donation. The boot of my car was packed with tinned goods, bread and packets of rice, and it took several trips to carry it all inside. As I entered the main passage from the dining room, slightly out of breath from the last load, a very tall person stood in front of me. She towered above me, thick-set in build, with broad shoulders and hands that hung large at her sides. She stopped me. I was a little startled. Then she spoke in broken English.

"I have been told to speak to you."

I said, "Sure. When would you like to speak to me?" I was eyeing the door for a quick escape. I had so much to do, and there was something about her presence that made the corridor feel smaller than it was.

"Now."

My heart sank. I looked at her and my instincts told me to be careful — perhaps her lack of personal space made me feel uneasy, or the wild look in her eyes, a look all too familiar from my years of psychiatric nursing — but my words said, "Let's go to the office." As we walked to the office, I sent up a silent prayer: Please, Lord, give me wisdom and confidence.

We sat next to each other on the settee. I had left the door slightly ajar, not wanting to lock myself in the office with her. The gap was perhaps six inches wide, enough to allow sound to carry into the passage should I need to call out. She began to say she needed my help.

"I am not safe."

At first I thought she was afraid and was in danger. That someone was threatening her, or that she was fleeing a situation. But then she explained that she could not trust herself not to harm anyone. The meaning shifted, and I felt a chill move through me despite the afternoon warmth. I could feel my feet restlessly shuffling next to each other. I shot a look at the door — it was still open. Her gaze followed mine. She had noticed. I felt uncomfortable. I kept quiet and nodded, giving her the cue to continue, showing that I was listening even as every nerve in my body urged me to leave.

She explained that she had an urgent desire to harm herself and others. The way she said it was clinical, almost detached, as though she were describing symptoms of a common illness. Then she told me that she had escaped from a high-security psychiatry unit in a different province and had been hiding in shelters, moving from one to another to avoid detection.

She had been committed to the high-security unit for life. As a child, she had committed arson. She had burnt down her boarding school, and the fire had resulted in the deaths of other children. She told me this without looking away. Her pale green eyes held mine, and I could see the torment in them. She could find no rest, she said, because she could hear the children screaming. It had started in her dreams, but now she could hear them during the day. The voices followed her from room to room, from shelter to shelter. They did not stop.

She had defaulted on her medication, and this was likely the contributing factor to the voices returning with such force. I looked into her pale green, pleading eyes. She looked as though she was in her mid-twenties. Her face looked worn from lack of sleep, the skin beneath her eyes bruised with exhaustion. One could see she was struggling. There was a tremor in her hands that she tried to still by pressing them together.

I asked her what she thought the best outcome would be for her. I chose the question deliberately, wanting her to feel that she had agency in whatever came next. Of her own accord, she admitted that she needed to be re-sectioned to the psychiatric unit, that she was too unstable and too erratic, and could easily kill again. She said those words — "kill again" — and I felt the weight of them settle over both of us.

I took a deep breath. I knew I had to choose my words very carefully so as not to trigger her. Years of psychiatric training and working with mentally challenged individuals had taught me to stay calm, to keep my voice even, to give nothing away in my posture or expression that might be read as a threat. I asked her what she would like me to do, and she said she wanted me to get her back into hospital. I agreed to write a referral letter which she could take to the local A&E department. They would arrange an emergency admission to the psychiatric ward. She agreed. There was relief on her face when I said yes — not joy, but the quiet relief of someone who knows they cannot save themselves and has found a person willing to help.

We parted ways, and as I climbed into the car, I realised that I had been in a very precarious situation. My hands shook slightly as I gripped the steering wheel. I thanked God for protecting me and giving me the correct words to say. The wrong word, the wrong tone, could have provoked a very different outcome. The following day, I returned with the referral letter. True to her word, she took herself off to the hospital and was admitted as an emergency to the psychiatric ward. I never heard from her again. But I have not forgotten her, and I hope that wherever she is, she has found some measure of peace.

Once again, I became acutely aware of God's protection over me and how He had placed me in the shelter to help His people. No matter what the situation was, I did not have to fear, as God was with me.

Chapter Nine

Ridge Haven

James 2:26: "Faith without deeds is dead."

2018 — I was becoming restless. It had been five years that I had been volunteering at The Nest. I was feeling that my tenure there had come to an end. It was a strange feeling, as though a season was closing and something new was beginning to stir, though I could not yet see its shape. Soswa had been to visit me, and I spoke with him about the elderly that were arriving at The Nest. They were vulnerable and I was concerned for their safety.

I was devastated to see how families dropped their elderly folk off on the pavement outside the shelter door and left them — and their suitcase or a bag — and took off with their social security card. The old person would stand there, blinking in the sunlight, watching the car that had brought them disappear down the road. Some wept. Some did not. The ones who did not weep were harder to look at. A few people were too embarrassed to tell their families, who had immigrated to a different country, that they were struggling financially, and would rather keep quiet and live in a shelter than admit they needed help.

After Soswa left, I was sitting in the sitting room having a cup of tea and chatting to God. I felt disturbed, and a thought entered my mind: open a home for the homeless elderly. Where did that come from? I could not open a shelter — it seemed complicated, overwhelming, would I have the capabilities needed? I prayed about it and the thought became stronger and clearer, refusing to be set aside.

Ross arrived home from work, and I casually said to him that God had a project for us. He came and sat down. His interest had been piqued. I told him that we were to open a home for the homeless elderly. He looked surprised. "Are you sure? That is a huge undertaking. Where would we even begin? I think you need to double-check and ask God again." I did, and the answer was the same.

After dinner I sat down at my computer. I had decided just to have a "look" at the properties available to rent. I had saved a nest egg and could afford a small monthly rental until the home could pay its own way. I had clicked on a few properties when one popped up. I could not believe the price — right in my budget range and in a good area, far away from the dangerous part of town where all the shelters were. I was excited. I sent the agent a message, not expecting a reply as it was late. Within minutes my phone pinged. The agent was available to meet me at the house the following morning at eight. I put the phone down and looked at Ross. Things were moving faster than either of us had anticipated.

The following morning I headed out with a hopeful heart. I met the agent and we went through the property. It was an old Jewish synagogue on the ground floor, and upstairs was the rabbi's home. It had a private garden down a long driveway, and the property could not be seen from the road, ensuring privacy. The rooms were generous, the ceilings high, and there was a quiet dignity to the building that felt appropriate for what we were planning. It was perfect.

I phoned Ross and asked him if he had some time to pop in during the day to check the physical building and to look at the double garage area and advise me as to whether it could be converted into a dormitory for the men. Ross did just that on his way home from work. He was very excited at what he saw and offered to arrange the renovation and pay for it as his contribution toward the project. It felt surreal. Was this truly going to go ahead?

It was a long weekend, and I took the time to phone twelve individuals to ask them if they would agree to be on the Ridge Haven board — Ross came up with the name. Every person I phoned was agreeable. Not one declined. They were professional men and women, the majority of whom were Christians. We agreed to meet at the property on the Monday morning to take a walk through and to have our first official meeting. I invited Soswa to join us.

Monday arrived and everyone met each other for the first time. We walked through the house with the agent, and it was unanimous: we should sign the lease agreement. I committed to start the process of registering Ridge Haven as a non-profit organization. I had the experience, as I had done the application for The Nest. Soswa was enthusiastic and offered spare beds. Ross was going to phone a contractor, and each board member offered to assist with different tasks. There was an energy in the room that morning that I had not expected. It felt as though something had been set in motion that was larger than any of us.

I asked the agent to prepare the lease agreement and went home to start the registration process for the non-profit organization. The duration of registration had changed, and I was told it could take up to a year. I continued regardless. This was God's project, and I was going to give it my all. I completed the application, gathered all the required documents — including identification documents from the board members, their signatures, the minutes of the first meeting, and a constitution. Just before five o'clock, close of business, I sent off the application via the Department of Social Development's website.

The following morning, I received an email acknowledging that my application had been received, and the following day we received our registration number. I was shocked. The registration was complete. It had been processed unbelievably quickly — a process that was supposed to take up to a year had taken two days. This was truly a God intervention. This gave me the certainty that the project was God's will.

I then went off with the certificate to the lawyer to sign the lease agreement. The lawyer advised the homeowner not to sign the agreement in the name of a non-profit. I was so disappointed — they had had their fingers burned previously where an NPO had not paid them and they had to evict them. I signed in my personal capacity. I was not going to let this little bump in the road stop us. The document was signed. It was really happening.

I drew up a timeline as to when everything needed to be ready. I wanted to have an Open Day two weeks from the date of signing. We had a lot to do. Ross had arranged for the contractor and he could start immediately. Darren, my son-in-law, arrived with his crew and offered to assist with equipping a new bathroom at his own expense. I made flyers to hand out to disabled and elderly people on the street and in shelters. I recruited a few younger women living in a shelter to help me hand them out. One of the board members took it upon herself to get the overgrown garden sorted out. The driveway, which had been choked with weeds, was cleared. The windows were washed. Slowly, the building began to look like a place where people might want to live.

All seemed to be going so well. Then I popped into The Nest to see Soswa. He was so angry. His manager had convinced him that I was a rival and that I was "taking food from his mouth" — the shelter was very much a business for him. I was shocked and saddened. He was furious that flyers had been handed out. My heart was broken. We had always had a good relationship. I had helped him register his own organization, had fundraised alongside him, had spent years building trust. And now a whisper from his manager had undone all of that. I went home totally unsure. I did not want a full-scale war with shelter bosses. I prayed about it, and God said to continue. I did.

The phone never stopped pinging as people were requesting to attend the Open Day. I would go through every day to clean and paint. A group of us assembled to get things done. One afternoon whilst I was up a ladder, paintbrush in hand, I heard women's voices coming down the driveway. A group of women from a Muslim charity had arrived. To this day I am not sure how they heard about us. They asked if there was any way in which they could help. They took a walk around, assessing what was needed with the practised eyes of people who had done this kind of work before, and then committed to come back and help us set up on the Open Day.

I dipped into my nest egg and ordered beds and mattresses, as Soswa was no longer amenable to giving us any.

Then the death threats started coming through. Shelter owners threatened my life if I took any of their residents. It was a thriving business for them, and every resident who left was money lost. I popped into The Nest in the hope of seeing Soswa, and he was not there, but the manager ordered a big, burly man to threaten to throw me down the front staircase. He also threatened that if I ever returned, he would ensure I would not see the light of day again. He started telling the elderly residents that I wanted to imprison them and make slaves of them — trying to create as much fear as possible. It was working among the residents to a certain extent. The people I had come to help were being turned against me by the very people who were supposed to be caring for them.

The Open Day eventually arrived, and we arranged to shuttle the homeless in our cars. Those living in shelters would meet us a few blocks away from their shelter, out of sight of the managers. Early on the morning of the Open Day, the Muslim women who had come to visit stayed true to their word. They arrived with dining room tables and chairs, tablecloths, and enough food to feed all our visitors, along with crockery and cutlery which they donated to us. We had received linen and curtains and a lounge suite from incredibly generous donors. The entire house came together from the generosity of individuals in the community.

The Jewish community also pulled together and assisted with donations. I had approached various churches within the immediate location of Ridge Haven, and sadly they were not forthcoming. My closest Christian friends, whom I thought would support our project, did not — and yet perfect strangers rallied to help where they could. It was a lesson that stayed with me. Generosity does not always come from the direction you expect.

We met with each person that came to the Open Day, and each went through an interview process. We explained the ethos of the home and the rules that would be implemented. After living on the street with no rules, this would eventually prove to be quite a challenge for some to adhere to.

The day was meant to be an introduction to Ridge Haven, and we only planned on taking people in two weeks later. When it came time to go home, there were so many tears and people begging us to allow them to stay. My heart broke. I looked at their faces — tired, hopeful, afraid — and I could not bring myself to send them back to the streets. We could house thirty people in total, and by the end of the week we had a house of thirty people. We shuttled up and down in our cars, daily helping bring people and their belongings to their new home.

Ross was bringing a group back to the house, and as they approached the gate, one of them spotted the postbox. She was so excited. "We have a postbox! Can we receive mail?" Such a simple thing, and yet it meant the world to the residents. As soon as they had a mailbox and an address, they could open a bank account. They were no longer homeless. They truly had a home, a community, and a family. I stood by the gate and watched her run her fingers over the number on the postbox, and I understood that dignity lives in the smallest details.

Each person that arrived had to have a full bath. All their belongings had to be disinfected and clothing washed due to the bed bugs in the shelter and the outbreak of scabies and lice. This all took time, and we gratefully accepted a big washing machine from a very kind donor.

The Muslim ladies had prepared special welcome gift packs of toiletries, biscuits and chocolates for each person, which they received on arrival. They felt as though they had arrived at the Ritz — and yet by our standards it was very basic accommodation. For those who had been living rough on the street, a plate of food and running hot water was such a luxury. I assisted an elderly man to the bathroom. He was nervous and reluctant at first. The daily grime of life had settled well onto his body. His frail skin, a tinge of grey- brown, the signature of a rough lived life. With some urging and encouragement, he eventually conceded and stepped under the running water. He stood under the shower for nearly twenty minutes, just letting the water run over him, eventually he came out of the bathroom and the gratitude on his face was like a warm embrace.

In the midst of the hustle and bustle of settling everyone into their new home I received a call from a sales rep visiting a client on a construction site. A lady in the admin department asked to speak to him. He had got to know her quite well over the years. She told him that she had gone down to the bottom of the yard and was checking up on inventory. She entered one of the shipping containers only to find an elderly man lying on the floor of the container. He was dehydrated, unkempt and appeared to have paralysis on the left side of his body. He could barely speak or open his eyes. Neither of them knew what to do with him. They asked if they could bring him across to Ridge Haven. I agreed.

About an hour later a car arrived with the elderly gentleman. His clothes were soiled. He had no form of identification or any belongings. We took him in. His face was ashen in color and very drawn. We had no idea how many days he had been lying in the container.

We took care of him and slowly we started to see an improvement. My years of nursing came in handy. Having worked alongside physiotherapists for years in ICU I was able to teach the carer which exercises to do to strengthen Gerald's left side. We eventually got to know his name as his speech improved. I bought a tennis ball so that he could squeeze it with his left hand to strengthen his muscles. Gerald eventually was able to get up and move around aided. The day he was able to climb the few stairs to the dining room with the help of the carer was a joyous occasion.

All the residents took turns to help him. We discovered that his daughter-in-law did not like him and when he had a stroke she arranged for him to be dumped in the container. She had made off with his social security card and his identity book. Gerald found a home at Ridge Haven. He found love and care. Initially he was a grumpy and hurt man, physically and emotionally. He eventually became a ray of sunshine that everyone chose to spend time with. His broken body and broken spirit healed. After a year we were able to help him down a path of forgiveness. He forgave his family for their neglect and for discarding him like an old rag. He eventually connected with his son again. The human spirit is truly remarkable and strong when given a chance.

The first meal together was an eye-opener. They were still in survival mode — every man for himself. They gulped the food down as if this might be the last meal for a while. Some wrapped bread in napkins and hid it under their chairs. We had to start small educational programmes, re-teaching the residents simple table etiquette and general manners toward each other. Some were afraid to bathe, and I had to check that they did. I had to watch them to ensure they did not sell their toiletries for extra money, as they had done when trying to survive on the streets. The habits of survival do not disappear overnight. They are written into the body, and it takes patience and time and gentleness to replace them with something new.

Once again I learned that through obedience and faith we witnessed God's love and blessings shower down on each member of the team, on the residents, and on the home. We walked closely with God and relied solely on Him. He directed our paths and helped us create a space worthy to be called their home. The residents experienced firsthand God's grace. We never forced Christianity on anyone, and the home was open to all — not just Christians. We saw lives change physically and spiritually.

It was a transient home, and we would eventually have a total of one hundred people move through it. We would help them heal by addressing their trauma. We were able to reconcile individuals with their families and find permanent retirement homes for them. We taught them to give back to the community and started our own outreach team. They loved it. They would go out to the street or shelters with me, with clothing and big pots of food which they would make during the day. They would show me where their younger friends were living, trying to survive, and we were able to help them in different ways. These outings were usually initiated by me, and then one day I received a call. The residents wanted to speak to me. World

Poverty Day was coming up and they had decided among themselves that they would like to fast on that day and donate their lunchtime sandwiches to the less fortunate. They all wanted to make the sandwiches themselves. We all gathered in the dining room — men and women together — armed with butter knives, butter, jam and loaves of bread. There was such joy as they sang and chatted whilst they each made their sandwiches. I had placed a wooden cross on a table in the dining room with a lit candle, and when each person had wrapped the sandwich they had made, they placed it at the foot of the cross. When everyone had completed their "love task," we gathered together to pray. Each thanked God for their own blessings and we prayed over the sandwiches, asking God to nourish and bless each person that received one. With great enthusiasm, one of the board members and I set off with a group in our cars. It was pouring with rain but spirits were not dampened by the weather. Each person was so excited to share the sandwiches that had been made. We stopped at traffic lights and handed sandwiches to those begging. A young man in a wheelchair sat on the side of the road with his mother. One of our ladies was so excited, as she knew them, and scuttled out of the car with a cheerful smile and handed over her little parcel. We found people who had taken shelter from the rain under bushes, in bus shelters, in parks and under bridges. That experience changed our residents that day. It was a turning point for all of them. They were no longer the ones receiving. They were giving. This newly learned gift of giving changed the dynamic in the home. People became more caring, looking out for those who may not have something. Their caring toward board members became evident. They started to see us in a different light. We were not merely the hand that fed them. They became partners with us.

These acts of kindness were soon put into practice once again. The police arrived at Ridge Haven and asked if we had a spare bed open. They had found a lady who had been left on the pavement with her suitcase in a very wealthy suburb of Durban known as Umhlanga Rocks. Her family had chased her from their home. Unfortunately we did not have a bed. They said they would take her downtown to a shelter.

That night I tossed and turned in my bed. I could not sleep. The thought of the frail old lady having to stay in a shelter upset me. She looked so vulnerable. The next morning I went to Ridge Haven and tried to work out a way of squeezing another bed into one of the rooms. It was a bit of a jigsaw puzzle but eventually the bed fitted and we were able to make a welcoming space for her.

I briefed the residents before I left and I told them that I would be fetching the lady from a shelter. I explained that she needed a lot of care and love from everyone as she had undergone severe trauma and abuse.

I went off to collect her. It was heartbreaking when I arrived at the shelter. I found her huddled on her bed clutching her bag. She looked so afraid. She struggled to walk as she had been beaten and her right leg dragged as she walked. I eventually managed to get her comfortable in the car and we set off to Ridge Haven. Abuse is not limited to one social strata.

On our arrival nothing prepared me for what was awaiting us. There were a small group of residents, men and women, in the car park waiting to welcome her. The men helped carry her case and a bag. Everyone shook her hand or hugged her. She was escorted to her room. An elderly lady, all bent over and crumpled herself, arrived with the biggest smile and a warm cup of tea. One by one residents popped their heads in. Each brought a little gift – a bar of soap, a tube of toothpaste, a face cloth, a chocolate bar. I held back the tears as I witnessed this miracle of love pouring out over a perfect stranger. The lessons we had tried to instill of kindness, love, 'that it is better to give than receive', were playing out with such beauty right before my eyes. God's love in action. To see people so willing to share what little they had with a stranger made my heart overflow with gratitude. That moment has imprinted itself in my memory forever. It reminded me of the story in the Bible of the widow who gave the last coin she owned. When people feel loved and cared for they are no longer guarded and in survival mode. They too are able to love and care for others. The Ridge Haven residents were a living testament of this.

The home became a true haven of joy and peace. New residents who arrived directly from the streets would find a group of people who poured out love and comfort. They were willing to share all they had. This was a true change. God had worked on each of their hard hearts and softened them.

One evening one of the residents stood on the deck and looked out over the city. As I stepped onto the deck she smiled. "Oh, how high I have come" she sighed. It was a sigh of relief and contentment. She pointed toward the city lights. "I can see where I used to live, right down there." She pointed her finger in the direction where the shelter was, close to the harbour. "God has lifted me high above all the pain, tears and fear."

Ridge Haven has left a mark on our hearts and in our lives.

"An Ode to Ridge Haven:"

The shimmering lights of Durban twinkle and sparkle below; I can pinpoint where I used to live in a shelter, oh so low.

Where rats would freely skelter and bed bugs dance on my frail frame at night — No rest for my weary head.

Thugs would prey, always ready to pounce. Every ounce of my body gripped with fear, As I would peer from my dark corner.

Oh God, where are you — come near. Do you hear my plea or see my tear?

Now my world has changed; to think I am worthy to have been rescued from such peril. It is clear that God is near.

Oh, Ridge Haven, how I smile.

I have never felt such love. As if I have been lifted on wings of a dove, Up high and far away from what I know.

Calmness and peace.

High above a world so fierce.

Here I stand — ascended. A new birth. No more fear; no more tear.

God, you truly hear. Thank you.

Chapter Ten

Trust In God

Jeremiah 17:7 "But blessed is the one who trusts in the Lord, whose confidence is in him."

God wants our bodies to be healed and whole. If we trust God, He can heal relationships, physical and mental illnesses. He can direct us when we are confused, uncertain, or need to make decisions. He does not promise us a life without struggle. What He promises is that He will walk through every struggle beside us, and that His purpose will prevail.

My life has been a testament to this. When I look back, my autoimmune disease was always present, creating debilitating health conditions, and yet even in the most challenging times, God was there. Not distant. Not silent. Present, faithful, and at work in ways I could not always see or understand in the moment, but which I would come to recognise only in hindsight.

In my late teens and early twenties, I had decided to train as a nurse. It felt like a calling more than a career choice. I wanted to be useful. I wanted to care for people. I had no idea then how profoundly that calling would shape the rest of my life, or what it would cost me.

1992. I was doing a stint on the paediatric ward when we received a call that changed the atmosphere of the entire unit in an instant. An entire village had been burnt during tribal warfare. Seven children under the age of six years were being brought to the hospital with burn injuries. We prepared as best we could. Nothing, however, can fully prepare you for what it looks like when children have been caught in that kind of violence.

I was on duty when they arrived. All little black, Zulu-speaking children, their small bodies bearing wounds that should never have been found on anyone. My heart ached when I saw the state they were in. The ward was quiet in the way that wards go quiet when something is too grave for ordinary noise.

I was assigned to a six-year-old girl. As I approached her bed, I could see her eyes widen. She was in pain and she was afraid, and she did not know me. Her gaze tracked my every movement with a wariness that broke something in me. We had carefully cleaned her wounds and bandaged her entire body. She was wrapped from head to toe, only her face and the area beneath her arms left exposed, the only skin the fire had not reached.

She needed the commode. I wheeled it in beside her bed. The problem was that I could not speak Zulu, and she could not speak English. There were no words between us, only gestures and the universal language of a nurse trying to communicate gentleness through her hands. I went to lift her out of bed, sliding my hands carefully beneath her arms, the one place I could hold her without causing pain. The moment she felt herself lifted, she startled. Her small body lurched. I caught her before she could fall face-first onto the floor, steadying her against me, but the sudden twist and pull sent a sharp sensation through my lower back. I heard something click. It was brief. I straightened up, settled her, and thought very little of it. There was too much to do.

That evening, when I went to assist another child in the bath, I bent forward over the tub and was stopped in my tracks by a pain so overwhelming and so sudden that I lost my breath entirely. My back locked. I could not move at all. I stood there, bent at the waist, unable to straighten, unable to reach anyone. Thankfully, there was a call bell string within reach. I pulled it and waited.

What appeared a simple injury would change the course of my life forever.

Over the following weeks, something more sinister began to unfold. I started to lose sensation in my legs gradually, so gradually at first that I questioned whether I was imagining it. Then it became undeniable. The pain in my back was excruciating and unrelenting. Breathing became slow and laboured, each breath a conscious effort rather than a reflex. I was referred to a neurosurgeon who was of the opinion that my symptoms were unrelated to the nursing incident. After a thorough evaluation, he diagnosed me with Guillain-Barré Syndrome, a condition in which the body's own immune system attacks the nervous system. It explained the ascending weakness, the loss of sensation, the difficulty breathing. It did not, however, explain what lay ahead of me emotionally.

I was two weeks away from sitting my final nursing exams. Our graduation ball was imminent. Ahead of me had been a finish line I had been running toward for years, and I had arrived at it unable to stand.

It was grad night. The girls were so excited. They had been speaking of this event for weeks, their voices bright with anticipation each time the subject came up. Dresses had been chosen, hair appointments made, shoes compared. They arranged, with characteristic kindness, to have pre-drinks in my hospital ward so that I would not miss the beginning of the evening entirely. They all arrived in their beautiful ball gowns, a procession of silk and sequins and perfume filling the antiseptic air of the ward. I fought back the tears. We had all worked so hard to reach this point in our lives, and here I was, flat on my back, watching them leave for a night I had imagined being part of for as long as I could remember.

After they had gone, the ward felt very quiet.

Not long after, my principal from the college came to see me. She stood at the end of my bed, a chubby woman with rosy cheeks and a rather stern character, not given to softening difficult truths with unnecessary kindness. She cleared her throat. Then, very matter-of-fact, she broke the news that there was a strong possibility I would never walk again. She let the words settle. "If you can ever stand again," she said, "phone me, and I will arrange for you to write your exams." With that, she marched out of my ward.

I lay there in the silence after she left. I was in shock, and yet I did not shed any tears. Instead, something quieter and more stubborn rose up in me. A determination I did not know I had until that moment. I thought: *that is what you think. I have God on my side.*

I was sent to my parents' home to recover. I could not use a walking frame because my arms could not support me. I was dependent on others for everything, which for a person who had trained precisely in order to care for others was a particular kind of humbling. My family gathered around me and held me up in every way they could.

One afternoon, my father walked into my room. He stopped when he saw me. I was lying flat on my back with study books propped up on my chest, reading. He asked me what I was doing. I told him I was studying for my exams. I was going to write. That was not in question in my mind.

He looked at me for a long moment. Then he reached down and placed his hand gently on my head and began to pray. He was the Anglican priest of a church in a small coastal town and a man of extraordinary faith, the kind that did not waver in the face of what the eye could see. He prayed quietly and at length, and then he went off to have his dinner.

A few days later, pins and needles began to move through my fingers. Slowly, almost imperceptibly at first, the use of my arms began to return. Then my toes started to twitch. The feeling crept back through my limbs like warmth returning to cold hands held near a fire. It was gradual and unmistakable. God had answered my father's prayers.

Eventually, I could log roll in bed and push myself upright to stand beside it. The moment I could stand, I phoned the college.

The principal was astonished. We arranged a time for me to come in and write.

I was ready.

My parents helped me into the college on the day of the exam. I shuffled slowly down the passage, my back still rigid and protesting every step. When the principal saw me approach, she looked genuinely taken aback. "But you can't sit," she said.

I looked at her steadily. "You said as soon as I could stand."

She stared at me. Then she picked up the phone and called the maintenance department. A jolly elderly man came up the stairs. She explained my dilemma to him with the no-nonsense efficiency that characterised her. He disappeared back down the stairs without a word of fuss and returned shortly after with two long straps and a drawing desk that could be tilted upright. He angled the desk to stand vertical, positioned me against it and secured me to it with the straps so that my back was fully supported. There I was: strapped to a tilted drawing board in the examination room, three hours of paper in front of me, and not a single doubt in my mind that I would finish it.

God gave me the strength and the willpower to see it through. I managed.

It would take a few more weeks before I was fully independent and able to care for myself again. My faith was strong, as was my belief in God. It was God and me, and together we would face the world. As had happened before, and as would happen again, there was no tidy medical explanation for the speed or completeness of my recovery. The doctors had no clear answers and offered no predictions. They were at a loss.

It would be twenty-four years later that we would discover it had all been connected to my APS: a diagnosis that, in retrospect, reframed so much of my history. What had seemed like isolated incidents, each one bewildering in its own way, were in fact threads of the same story. And through all of it, God had been present. Not removing the difficulty, but sustaining me through it, again and again, in ways that no medical chart could fully account for.

Chapter Eleven

In The Darkness

Isaiah 42:16 "I will bring the blind by a way they did not know; I will lead them in paths they have not known. I will make darkness light before them, and crooked things straight. These things I will do for them, and not forsake them."

There are moments in life when the ground shifts beneath you without warning. No tremor, no sign. You go to sleep in one world and wake in another. What follows is not a test of your strength. It is an invitation to discover whose strength you have actually been living on all along.

We had been living in Portugal for two years, a season of quiet rebuilding after the upheavals that had come before. The days had a gentleness to them that we had not always known, a slower rhythm, a different light. But the distance from those we loved most had not become easier with time. We had not seen our daughter in two years, held back from each other by COVID travel restrictions that had made the world feel at once very large and very small. Then, finally, it was 2023, and she was coming. She and her husband were flying in to spend Christmas with us, and the anticipation of it filled the house like warmth before a fire is even lit.

I went to bed that Friday evening full of excitement and in good health.

On Saturday morning I woke early. There were a few last preparations to see to before her arrival, small things I had been saving for the final days, the kind of details that make a homecoming feel intentional. I opened my eyes.

Everything was dark.

My first thought was entirely ordinary. I wondered whether we had closed the shutters the night before. When they are fully closed, they create a room as dark as a cave, the light sealed out completely. I lay still and waited for my eyes to adjust. They did not. The darkness held. I touched my face, pressed my fingertips lightly to my eyelids. They were open. I blinked. Still nothing. Not the soft dark of an unlit room, but an absolute absence of light that no amount of blinking or waiting would resolve.

It took a few minutes for the reality to take shape. I was blind.

I lay there for a moment in that realisation and did the only thing I knew to do instinctively. I prayed. Not at length, not with formulated words, but a quiet and immediate appeal: *God, keep me calm. Fill me with peace.* And He did. The fear that should have rushed in with a force equal to what I was facing instead held back, like a wave that draws up and does not break.

I felt Ross stir beside me. I reached out and said good morning, steadying my voice as carefully as I would steady my hand. He began to get out of bed. I told him, quietly, that I could not see. He came around to my side immediately. I could hear his footsteps on the floor, could hear him reach for the bedside lamp and click it on, but there was no corresponding shift in what I could perceive. Only when he asked me what I could see did I realise that the absolute blackness had shifted very slightly. It was no longer total. It was dark grey, the colour of a sky before dawn, but without any promise of sunrise. He helped me to the bathroom. We did not yet say aloud what we were both thinking.

I decided to wait until Monday before calling the doctor's rooms. I told myself it might pass, and I held that possibility close through the weekend. It did not pass. The darkness remained, unyielding and entire. On Monday, Ross phoned an ophthalmic surgeon, who agreed to see me within two days.

Those days were long in a way that is difficult to describe to someone who has not experienced sudden blindness. Time behaves differently when you cannot see it move. There is no glance at a clock, no change in the quality of light through a window to tell you the afternoon is fading. There is only the ongoing darkness and the sounds of the world continuing around you. I filled the silence with God. Verses I had memorised from the Bible as a child came back to me unbidden, surfacing from somewhere deeper than memory, and I let them speak. Surprisingly, I remained calm. I held onto the belief that this was transient. I did not know why I was so certain of it, but the certainty was there, solid and unearned, and I chose to stand on it.

The specialist gave us the news without cushioning it. My optic nerve was damaged. The loss of sight was irreversible. He could operate, but he could not promise any improvement. He spoke with the measured authority of a man who had delivered difficult truths many times and had learned not to soften them into something misleading.

I thanked him. We walked out.

On the pavement outside his consulting rooms, I turned to Ross and said: "I bind that in the name of Jesus. I do not receive that negative report. I don't believe this is forever. God will restore my eyesight. I know He will." Ross took my elbow and we stood there together on that ordinary pavement in Portugal, and we prayed. We handed it over. There is a particular kind of freedom in that act, not passivity, not denial, but a deliberate release of something too heavy to carry alone into hands equipped to hold it.

We went home to pack.

The next day we drove to Lisbon to collect Tammy and Darren from the airport. I had not told my daughter before she boarded the plane. I had not wanted to begin her holiday with worry, and I had not wanted to make my condition the centre of what should have been a joyful reunion. The moment she saw me, of course, she knew something was different. Mothers are not easily hidden from their children.

We had a trip planned. We were taking them north, up through the green and ancient landscape of Portugal. Darren wanted to see the Big Wave at Nazaré, that extraordinary stretch of Atlantic coastline where the ocean does something that oceanographers still find remarkable, where waves rise to heights that seem to belong to a different scale of nature entirely. I did not see it. I heard it. The sound of it, the deep concussive boom of water at that volume, was something I felt more than heard, a vibration that moved through the ground and through me.

I was learning, during those weeks, what blindness teaches that nothing else can. The other senses do not simply continue as before. They quicken and sharpen, as though the body, denied one avenue of information, throws its full resource into every other. Smells became vivid and precise. Sound sorted itself into layers I had never noticed. The texture of things under my hands, the temperature of air moving through a room, the taste of food I had eaten a hundred times, all of it arrived with a new and particular intensity. What also arrived, more quietly but no less powerfully, was humility. To need help getting dressed, to need a hand to move from one room to the next, to be unable to read a face or navigate a staircase alone, is to understand in your body what it means to be dependent. I had spent much of my life caring for others in exactly this kind of vulnerability. Now I inhabited it myself. It was not a comfortable lesson, but it was a true one.

Slowly, gradually, I began to perceive changes. The absolute dark shifted into an awareness of light and shade. Shades became shadows. Shadows became indistinct shapes, moving forms, ghostly and imprecise but present. I kept this to myself at first, afraid to name it in case naming it made it fragile.

Every morning I woke with the same prayer of thanks for healing taking place and the same hope: that today would be the day. Days became weeks. A month passed with little change. Then two months. Somewhere in the middle of all of it, I became aware that my master's programme was waiting for me.

The semester was due to begin again at the end of February. Ross and I talked about it at length, the two of us working through what was possible and what was not. I was not willing to abandon what I had built. Too much had been invested, too much ground covered, to stop now. We agreed that Ross would write as I dictated. It was not ideal. It was what we had, and it was enough.

I kept praying. I was not afraid. I had made a choice, conscious and deliberate, not to construct a future in my imagination in which I could not see. I did not picture that life. I did not let my mind move toward it. I believed, with everything in me, that God would heal me, and I kept my eyes, useless as they were, pointed toward that belief.

It was a Sunday in the third month. We were in church, and the worship had moved into a song I did not recognise, one I had not heard before. I lifted my head in the direction of the sound.

A bright flash of light came from outside, sudden and sharp, just as the congregation began to sing the words: *Christ is our light.*

The third verse of the song was about Christ being light for those who are homeless. The words found something in me before I had time to prepare for them. My mind moved immediately back to South Africa, back to the shelter, back to the faces of the people I had walked alongside in their darkness and their need. A tear moved down my face. Memory and music and something larger than both of them met in that moment.

I lifted my head.

I could see the screen.

The words we were singing were displayed on it, clear and legible, and I could read them. I could *see* them. Not shadows. Not shapes. Words. The room around me. The light.

God had restored my eyesight.

What followed was not a single emotion but a rush of many arriving at once: jubilation, disbelief, tears, laughter held quietly inside so as not to disturb the people around me still singing, and beneath all of it, a humbling so complete it had no bottom. His power and His mercy and His love and His grace all arrived together in that moment and fell over me like rain. I did not deserve it more than anyone else in that room. I had not earned it through the right combination of prayer or faith or goodness. It was simply given, in His timing, which is always perfect, and which almost never matches ours.

I was a week away from my new semester beginning.

I returned to the ophthalmic surgeon. He examined my eyes with the same careful thoroughness as before. When he was finished, he sat back and looked at me. The optic nerve was perfect. The tests showed no trace of the damage that had been there. There was no medical explanation for why I had lost my sight, and equally no medical explanation for why I had regained it. He had none to offer.

I did not need one.

I had declined the operation. I had taken no medication. What I had done was pray, and trust, and wait, and refuse to let my imagination build a life in the dark. That is not a formula. It is not a technique. It is simply faith, lived out day by day in the absence of evidence, until the evidence arrives.

I have so much to be grateful for. So much to give God thanks for. And I am aware, deeply and constantly, that the story is not finished.

Chapter Twelve

Conclusion

It is 2026.

Fourteen years have passed since my official diagnosis. In the early days after my first catastrophic event, various doctors told me that the survival rate for someone in my condition was approximately five years. I heard those words, filed them away, and continued to get up each morning. Fourteen years. I do not say that with any sense of triumph over medicine, or over the doctors who delivered those statistics in good faith. I say it with one hand open and my eyes turned upward, because I know with absolute certainty that those extra years were not earned. They were given.

Over the course of fifty-eight years, I have seen God's hand on my life in ways I could not have scripted or anticipated. I have seen it in the small and quiet moments: a stranger's kindness at precisely the right time, a verse surfacing from memory in the dark, a sense of peace arriving where panic had every right to be. I have seen it in the extraordinary: a back that unlocked when the doctors expected paralysis, a referral made on a nudge that turned into a shelter that changed dozens of lives, eyesight restored in a church on a Sunday morning without medication or surgery or any explanation that belongs to the natural world. He has been with me through every trial. Not hovering at a distance, observing. Present. Steady. Working.

He has also, in the way that those who love us most will do, demanded things of me. Obedience, when obedience was costly and the easier path was right there. Surrender, when my instinct was to hold on and manage things myself. Trust, when the circumstances gave me very little to base it on. Each time I brought Him my fear, He lifted it. Not always immediately, not always in the way I had imagined He would, but consistently and without fail. My faith has been tested in ways I would not have chosen. It has also grown in ways I could not have engineered. The two things are not unrelated.

I still have Antiphospholipid Syndrome. That has not changed and is unlikely to. Each day is a new exercise in navigating symptoms that shift and challenge, in reading my body with the particular attentiveness that chronic illness requires and that nobody asks for but many of us develop. There are mornings that are harder than others. There are days when the body makes demands that interrupt everything else, when plans are rearranged around what is possible rather than what is preferred.

This is the ordinary texture of a life lived with a condition that does not resolve. I do not romanticise it.

And yet each day also carries evidence of something else. The grace and mercy of God are not abstractions to me. They are daily realities, demonstrated in the gap between what my medical history suggests should be and what actually is. Each morning that I rise and function and think and love and pray and work is, when I hold it up to the light, a small miracle sitting quietly inside an ordinary day.

Does my faith get challenged? Most certainly. I would not trust the faith that had never been tested, just as I would not trust a bridge that had never borne any weight. There are moments when the struggle is acute and the silence feels long, when I ask God where He is and the answer does not come in the form I was hoping for. There are moments when I wonder — now and again, in the honesty of the small hours — whether the next challenge will be the one that is finally too much. Whether I have reached the edge of the miraculous. Whether this will be the time the answer is no.

And then the Holy Spirit, faithful as always, brings back the one thing that matters above all the rest: *He will never leave me or forsake me.* Not a feeling. A promise. And promises, I have found over fifty-eight years, are what hold when everything else gives way.

I will continue. That is not stubbornness, though I have that quality in some measure. It is a decision made and remade each morning, rooted in something more reliable than my own determination. I will continue as a warrior for the Lord, fighting the good fight, not because I am particularly brave or particularly strong, but because He equips those He calls and I have seen the evidence of that equipping too many times to doubt it now. I will serve Him as best I am able, within the limitations of the body I have been given, within the season I am in, within whatever capacity each day affords. And I will share His message of salvation whenever I can, because that message is not mine to keep.

The story of my life is not a story about survival, though survival features in it repeatedly. It is not a story about resilience, though I have had to reach for that resource more times than I can count. It is a story about what happens when an ordinary person, imperfect and frequently uncertain, places her hand inside the hand of an extraordinary God and keeps walking.

Just as a caterpillar retreats into its cocoon and returns transformed into a beautiful butterfly, God continues to transform my life into something beautiful. The cocoon is not a comfortable place. It is dark and confining and the creature inside it cannot see what is happening or what it is becoming.

But the darkness is not the end of the story. It is the necessary passage through which beauty arrives.

Whatever comes next, He goes ahead of me.

That is enough. That has always been enough.

About the Author

Dr Yvette Stembridge is a South African who has lived in the UK and now lives in Portugal with her husband Ross. She has various qualifications which include degrees in  Education, Nursing, Business, Marketing and a PhD in Philosophy majoring in Theology and Missiology.

She is the founder of Connect Women's Ministry in Portugal. Yvette is a trained pastor, missionary, speaker and counsellor. She is passionate about God, His people and cultures. In her free time she loves to travel, take long beach walks and to paint. Yvette can be contacted by email:yvettestembridge@gmail.com

Cup Cakes of Hope

An NPO that sponsors children with Cancer. Please donate to their work.
https://cupcakesofhope.org/

South Africa

EFT Bank Details
Account name:Cupcakes of HOPE
Nedbank Ltd
Branch:Three Rivers
Branch Code: 198765 or 193305
Account no:1028740565
Payments via Swift Code:NEDSZAJJ
Ref: B26name and contact number

United Kingdom

EFT Bank Details
Account name:Global Cupcakes of HOPE UK
Bank:CAF Bank
Cash Account Number:00033844
Sort Code:40-52-40
IBAN:GB18CAFB40524000033844
Ref:B26 Name & Contact number

Hands for Hearts, Durban, South Africa

An NPO that assists the community.
https://www.facebook.com/Handsforhearts.co.za/

Hands For Hearts

Bank: FNB
Account no: 62883516901
Branch Code: 220426
Swift Code: FIRNZAJJ